US IMMIGRATION
POLICY

BY A. R. CARSER

CONTENT CONSULTANT

GREGORY S. BACHMEIER
IMMIGRATION ATTORNEY
BACHMEIER LAW OFFICE

Essential Library

An Imprint of Abdo Publishing | abdopublishing.com

abdopublishing.com

Published by Abdo Publishing, a division of ABDO. PO Box 398166, Minneapolis,
Minnesota 55439. Copyright © 2018 by Abdo Consulting Group, Inc. International
copyrights reserved in all countries. No part of this book may be reproduced in
any form without written permission from the publisher. Essential Library™ is a
trademark and logo of Abdo Publishing.

Printed in the United States of America, North Mankato, Minnesota
092017
012018

Cover Photo: Stephan Savoia/AP Images
Interior Photos: Marcio Jose Sanchez/AP Images, 4–5; Geoff Forester/The Concord
Monitor/AP Images, 11; North Wind Picture Archives, 12–13, 62–63; Everett Historical/
Shutterstock Images, 18, 21, 72–73; AP Images, 23, 31; Peter J. Carroll/AP Images,
26–27; David Bundy/AP Images, 36; Glenn Fawcett/US Customs and Border
Protection, 40–41; Ashley Hopkinson/AP Images, 44; Reed Saxon/AP Images, 49,
71; Mohammad Hannon/AP Images, 51; Elaine Thompson/AP Images, 52–53; Heriberto
Rodriguez/MCT/Tribune News Service/Getty Images, 58; Ted S. Warren/AP Images,
66; Bruce Bisping/MCT/Newscom, 76; C. M. Guerrero/El Nuevo Herald/AP Images,
79; Jim West/Sipa Press/Newscom, 82–83; Ross D. Franklin/AP Images, 89; Rena
Schild/Shutterstock Images, 92–93; iStockphoto, 95; Arthur Greenberg/Shutterstock
Images, 97; Anthony Behar/Sipa USA/AP Images, 99

Editor: Melissa York
Series Designer: Maggie Villaume

Publisher's Cataloging-in-Publication Data

Names: Carser, A R., author.
Title: US immigration policy / by A. R. Carser.
Description: Minneapolis, Minnesota : Abdo Publishing, 2018. | Series: Special reports
    | Includes bibliographic references and index.
Identifiers: LCCN 2017946880 | ISBN 9781532113376 (lib.bdg.) | ISBN 9781532152252
    (ebook)
Subjects: LCSH: Emigration and immigration--Government policy--Juvenile literature.
    | United States--Juvenile literature.
Classification: DDC 325.73--dc23
LC record available at https://lccn.loc.gov/2017946880

CONTENTS

CHAPTER ONE

DANGEROUS WORK
REWARDED

T amim Ziaye was studying economics in an Afghan college in 2011 when the US military offered him a great opportunity. Ziaye could earn a consistent paycheck to support his education. The only catch was that his new job was incredibly dangerous. He would be translating for the US military in the Afghanistan War (2001–). Despite the threat of gunfire, explosions, and kidnapping, Ziaye worked side by side with US troops for two years.

A former Afghan interpreter for the US Army, Qismat Amin, *left*, arrived in the United States in February 2017 after waiting four years for his visa.

RESETTLING THE TRANSLATORS

Arriving in the United States after working and living in a war zone across the world can be disorienting and confusing. No One Left Behind is a nonprofit organization founded by a former US Army captain. The group provides translators and their families with housing, furniture, jobs, and transportation once they arrive in the United States. Between 2013 and 2017, the group helped 2,782 people resettle in the United States. But the group's work was far from done. More than 35,000 translators remained behind in Iraq and Afghanistan.[1]

In March 2014, Ziaye applied for a special immigrant visa available to individuals who translated for US troops in Iraq and Afghanistan. In exchange for their service, translators could petition the US Citizenship and Immigration Services (USCIS) to be allowed into the United States as lawful permanent residents. The process could take years. It required applicants to prove they worked as translators or interpreters for the US military. They had to pass background checks and obtain a letter of recommendation from an officer. Then, applicants were interviewed in person at a US embassy and waited for the application to be processed. Once admitted, translators received assistance relocating to the United States through the country's refugee program.

It took two years for Ziaye's visa application to be processed. But finally, March 15, 2016, arrived, and Ziaye moved from Afghanistan to Denver, Colorado, where he now works at the Denver airport. But many of his fellow interpreters are still in Afghanistan waiting for their visas. The program offers a limited number of visas per year to translators and interpreters. In March 2017, more than 10,000 applicants were in line for their paperwork to lawfully enter the United States as permanent residents.[2] The program has been caught in the middle of an ongoing political battle over the future of the country's immigration policy. "We have a bipartisan coalition in the House and Senate that are working to keep these people safe," said US Congressman Earl Blumenauer of Oregon in 2017. "Yet, Congress is still failing to do its job. It shouldn't be this hard."[3]

IMMIGRATION TERMINOLOGY

Congressman Blumenauer's frustration illustrates how difficult reforming the country's complex and extensive immigration program can be. Immigrants come from

"WHEN THEY UNDERSTAND HOW WE CAME TO THE US, HOW HARD WE WORK, HOW WE PUT OUR LIVES IN DANGER, THEY UNDERSTAND."[4]

—TAMIM ZIAYE, FORMER AFGHANI TRANSLATOR FOR THE US MILITARY, 2017 countries across the world for a variety of reasons. Some seek a career in a highly skilled industry. Others are fleeing political, religious, or ethnic oppression. Most immigrants come to the country legally through the visa program. A visa is a document that allows an immigrant to apply for entry into the United States. An Arrival/Departure Record documents the conditions of an immigrant's stay in the United States. Lawful permanent residents are individuals who have arrived lawfully on an immigrant visa. These immigrants are sometimes informally referred to as green card holders. Many lawful permanent residents come to the United States to reunite with a family member or to

WHAT IS A GREEN CARD?

Green card is a former name for the Permanent Lawful Resident Card that grants cardholders the right to live permanently in the United States. The first version of the card was called an Alien Registration Receipt. For many years the card was green in color. Many green card holders can apply to become naturalized after holding their green cards for five years and fulfilling a number of other requirements.

start a career or business in the United States. Others arrive as refugees or as immigrants from countries underrepresented in the United States.

Refugees are individuals who have fled persecution and turmoil in their home countries. They have left their home countries due to war, genocide, political oppression, or religious persecution. An asylee is a type of refugee, one who is already in the United States or who is seeking admission at a port of entry.

While most immigrants enter the country lawfully, some cross the border without applying for a visa or without the proper documentation. Others enter the United States lawfully on nonimmigrant, temporary visas but overstay the terms of their visas. In these situations, the individual is considered an unauthorized immigrant. The term for this class of immigrant has evolved over time and been the subject of debate among pro-immigration advocates and those calling for restricted immigration. *Illegal alien, illegal, illegal immigrant, undocumented immigrant,* or *unauthorized*

THE VISA PROCESS

Obtaining an immigrant visa is no easy feat. First, the immigrant files a petition to apply for a visa to the USCIS. The immigrant must have a sponsor already living or doing business in the United States. If the petition is approved, the immigrant fills out and submits the required forms to the National Visa Center. Next, the immigrant completes an in-person interview at a US embassy or consulate abroad. After the interview, the immigrant's application for a visa is approved or denied. If approved, the immigrant receives a packet of documents and the visa documentation in his or her passport. The immigrant presents the papers to the US Customs and Border Protection (CBP) agent when the immigrant arrives in the United States. The agent reviews the documents and admits the immigrant, who enters the United States as a lawful permanent resident.

immigrant all refer to someone who is in the United States without going through the visa application process. The US Department of Homeland Security (DHS), through US Immigration and Customs Enforcement (ICE), is responsible for identifying, arresting, and deporting unauthorized immigrants from the United States. Deportation is the formal removal of an unauthorized immigrant from the United States.

IMMIGRATION AND THE UNITED STATES

In 2015, 43.2 million immigrants lived in the United States, more immigrants than in any other country in the world. Of this number, approximately 11 million were unauthorized immigrants, or 25 percent. Approximately 44 percent of immigrants were naturalized citizens, while 5 percent were temporary residents and 26 percent were permanent residents.[5] Immigrants represented 13.5 percent of the US population, the highest percentage in nearly a century. Immigrants held 17 percent of jobs in the United States, up from 5 percent in 1970.[6]

Immigrants come from almost every country. People from Latin America comprise the largest group of immigrants who arrived in the United States between 2010 and 2014. But immigration from Saudi Arabia, Bangladesh, Iraq, Egypt, Pakistan, India, and Ethiopia increased the most during that time.

People have arrived on American shores seeking a better life since before the country was founded more than 240 years ago. Since then, experts, policymakers, political figures, and the American public have debated the best ways to allow immigrants into the country to benefit newcomers and strengthen American society.

Esther Elonga, a refugee who grew up in Congo and then Uganda, attended two years of high school in New Hampshire before being accepted at Harvard University in 2017.

"YOUR TIRED, YOUR POOR"

When Europeans set sail across the Atlantic Ocean to explore and establish colonies in North America, they encountered Native Americans who had called the continent home for tens of thousands of years. Over the 1500s and 1600s, Dutch, English, French, and Spanish explorers and colonists arrived in North America. Some Europeans tried to trade and establish a relationship with the Native American communities they encountered. Others acted with hostility and violence.

A variety of factors pushed Europeans to immigrate to North American colonies in this era. Some came to seek new economic opportunities in the New World, from farming in the English Virginia colonies to fur

The Pilgrims from England established their colony at Plymouth, Massachusetts, so they could practice their religion.

trading in New France and the Dutch colony of New Amsterdam. Others arrived on the shores of North America fleeing religious persecution. Puritans established the Massachusetts Bay Colony to avoid oppression by the Church of England. Jewish people immigrated to New Amsterdam seeking religious freedom. But they were met with hostility from the Dutch Reformed Church, which had a large presence in the colony. These Jewish immigrants overcame this animosity and established the first permanent Jewish community on the continent's East Coast.

"WE EAT HERE EVERY DAY WHAT WE GOT ONLY FOR EASTER IN OUR COUNTRY."[1]

—POLISH IMMIGRANT, 1880s

By the 1700s, immigration to the North American colonies was so popular that European and colonial governments began regulating it. The governments passed laws on the type of people allowed to immigrate. Despite these restrictions, people continued to emigrate from Europe in large numbers. By the late 1700s, more than 110,000 Germans had immigrated to Pennsylvania.[2] During the same time, up to 300,000 Irish and Scottish people immigrated to the English colonies, fleeing political upheaval and economic hardship.[3]

IMMIGRATION BETWEEN THE REVOLUTIONARY AND CIVIL WARS

Conflict on the North American continent cut back immigration during the American Revolution (1775–1783). In 1775, England prohibited all immigration to its North American colonies, and emigration from other European nations ceased to avoid the violence. But when the war ended, European immigrants began to travel to the newly formed United States. "The Bosom of America is open to receive not only the Opulent and respectable Stranger," proclaimed President George Washington, "but the oppressed and persecuted of all Nations and Religions."[4]

Washington's proclamation was the first step in creating the vision of the United States as a refuge for people who sought economic, political, and religious freedom. In 1790, the first census revealed that nearly two-thirds of the white population in the United States had immigrated from or were descendants of immigrants from England, Scotland, Ireland, and Wales. One-fifth of the entire country's population were slaves who had been taken from Africa against their will or were descendants of people who endured this forced migration.[5] The census did not include Native Americans. That same year, on March 26, the US Congress passed the country's first Naturalization Act. Immigrants who lived in the United States for two years became naturalized citizens. The law was changed in 1795 to increase this time to five years.

Over the next five decades, people from around the world immigrated in large numbers to the United States. Americans and immigrants alike were attracted to the opportunity that lay in westward expansion past the Appalachian Mountains. While newly arrived immigrants from Germany, Ireland, and Scandinavia migrated west, the US government systematically began pushing Native Americans off their lands by treaty and by force.

Another group of immigrants came to the United States in the first half of the 1800s, arriving on the Pacific coast from China. Similar to their European counterparts moving west from the East Coast, Chinese immigrants sought economic opportunity in the western territories. The labor of many Chinese immigrants was vital to

MORE TO THE
STORY

THE SLAVE TRADE

Over the course of more than three centuries, approximately 12.5 million people were forcibly taken from their homelands in Africa. Men, women, and children were kidnapped and sold into slavery, forced to travel across the Atlantic Ocean in horrendous conditions that many did not survive. Historians estimate approximately 10.7 million enslaved people arrived in the Americas, where they were enslaved by white Europeans.[6] Survivors farmed some of the world's most valuable commodity crops—tobacco, cotton, and sugar—enriching their enslavers.

In the early 1600s, Africans forced to migrate to the colonies of North America were considered indentured servants who worked under contract for European landowners. Once their contracts were up, indentured servants became free to find other employment and own land. But by 1640, this system had broken down. European colonists began to see free Africans as a threat to their prosperity. In 1641, Massachusetts became the first colony to recognize slavery. By the mid-1700s, up to 45,000 Africans were removed to the Americas every year.[7] Congress prohibited the forced migration of slaves from Africa to the United States in 1807. But the legal practice of slavery continued for more than half a century after that.

building the country's railroad network. Despite these
contributions, immigrants from China faced growing
anti-immigrant sentiment from the American public,
as did the Irish immigrants who were arriving in the
country in great numbers to flee the Irish Potato Famine.
By the 1850s, this nativist feeling had organized into
the Know-Nothing Party, whose members feared
immigrants would compete for their jobs. They felt
the majority-Protestant country was threatened by the
Catholic beliefs of many European newcomers.

Irish immigrants arriving in New York by ship, 1855

THE IMMIGRATION BOOM: 1880 TO 1917

During the American Civil War (1861–1865), conflict in the United States once again curbed immigration. After the war, immigration rapidly increased. From 1865 to 1917, more than 27.3 million people immigrated to the United States.[8] The majority came from European countries such as Austria-Hungary, Germany, Ireland, and Italy. But many others emigrated from Asian and Middle Eastern countries such as China, Japan, and Turkey.

Whether they came alone or with their families, newcomers brought new languages, traditions, skills, and religions to the United States. Many of the immigrants coming to the country in the early 1900s were fleeing

PORTS OF ENTRY

How and where immigrants enter the United States has changed over the country's history. In the early days of the United States, immigrants freely entered the country through its port cities. Castle Garden in New York City processed new European arrivals between 1855 and 1890. It was the busiest entry point in the country during that time, handling more than two-thirds of the country's immigrants.[9] But as immigration increased in the late 1800s, the federal government established several immigration stations. Ellis Island opened its doors in 1892. It would process more than one-half of all immigrants to the United States by the time it closed 62 years later.[10] On the West Coast, Angel Island in San Francisco, California, processed hundreds of thousands of immigrants from Asia from 1910 to 1940. As airplanes overtook travel by ocean liner, airports across the country became hubs for immigrants entering the country. Today, every state in the nation is a port of entry.

oppressive monarchies and depressed economies. Others were ethnic or religious minorities who were persecuted in their native countries.

As the number of new immigrants rose, many Americans had increasingly negative perceptions of the newcomers, though many citizens were immigrants or descendants of immigrants themselves. Another wave of nativism broke out across the country. Labor unions worried the new immigrants would be willing to work for less than their American counterparts, thus stealing American jobs. Others worried the unfamiliar religions of some immigrants would start to dominate American culture. And politicians were worried immigrants from Germany and Russia would threaten democracy with communist or anarchist beliefs.

The dramatic increase in immigration during this time showed the need for an organized federal immigration system. The anti-immigrant

"*RESOLVED*, THAT FOREIGN IMMIGRATION, WHICH IN THE PAST HAS ADDED SO MUCH TO THE WEALTH, DEVELOPMENT OF RESOURCES AND INCREASE OF POWER TO THE NATION, THE ASYLUM OF THE OPPRESSED OF ALL NATIONS, SHALL BE FOSTERED AND ENCOURAGED BY A LIBERAL AND JUST POLICY."[11]

—PLATFORM OF THE REPUBLICAN PARTY, FORMULATED IN PART BY ABRAHAM LINCOLN, 1864 sentiment that was rising among the American public would influence several new immigration laws. Before the 1880s, the federal government did little to regulate immigration to the United States. Immigration was generally open, and most rules were left up to the states. But the growing immigrant population and anti-immigrant sentiment led to the creation of the country's first federal law to regulate immigration in 1882. That year, Congress passed the Chinese Exclusion Act, the first federal law to broadly restrict most immigration from a particular country. The law was extended by several acts of Congress. In 1902, it was expanded to include immigrants from the

At the turn of the 1900s, immigrants crowded into New York neighborhoods such as Little Italy.

Philippines and Hawaii. The restrictive act faced opposition from Chinese-born immigrants and Chinese Americans and strained the relationship between the United States and China, but it was not repealed until 1943.

Other laws enacted between the 1880s and World War I (1914–1918) gave the federal government the power to restrict immigration for

> "GIVE ME YOUR TIRED, YOUR POOR, YOUR HUDDLED MASSES YEARNING TO BREATHE FREE, THE WRETCHED REFUSE OF YOUR TEEMING SHORE. SEND THESE, THE HOMELESS, TEMPEST-TOST TO ME, I LIFT MY LAMP BESIDE THE GOLDEN DOOR!"[12]
>
> —EMMA LAZARUS, "THE NEW COLOSSUS," 1883, AS ENGRAVED ON THE STATUE OF LIBERTY

certain groups of people and to tax immigrants when they entered the United States. The 1891 Immigration Act federalized the country's immigration system. It established the Bureau of Immigration, tasked with executing most immigration laws, regulating inspections of immigrants taking place along the US border, and deporting immigrants who entered the country without authorization. Subsequent laws expanded and clarified the rules and restrictions in the 1891 act.

The Angel Island immigration station in San Francisco, California, received immigrants mostly from China and Japan from 1910 to 1940.

IMMIGRATION BETWEEN THE WORLD WARS

As with the American Revolution and Civil War before it, World War I caused a dramatic decrease in immigration. In 1914, the year the war began, 1.2 million people immigrated to the United States. The next year, just 326,700 did.[13] Immigration remained low in the years after the war, too, due to increasingly restrictive federal laws. The era of mass immigration had come to an end.

Over the course of the 1920s, several new laws slowed immigration to a trickle. It would not pick up until after World War II (1939–1945). The 1921 Emergency Quota Law created a system that allowed only a certain number of people to immigrate from a particular country. Generally, the quotas favored immigration from western Europe, especially the United Kingdom and France. It restricted immigration from countries in eastern Europe and southern Europe, such as Italy and the newly created Soviet Union. Three years later, Congress passed the Johnson-Reed Act, which set up the country's first visa system. The system required immigrants to obtain a visa to enter the United States before arriving in the country. When the Great Depression threw the United States and the world into economic turmoil in 1929, immigration numbers decreased further.

"I SAY THE CLASS OF IMMIGRANTS COMING TO THE SHORES OF THE UNITED STATES AT THIS TIME ARE NOT THE KIND OF PEOPLE WE WANT AS CITIZENS OF THIS COUNTRY."[14]

—REPRESENTATIVE JAMES V. MCCLINTIC (D-OK) IN AN ADDRESS TO CONGRESS, 1921

In the years before World War II, US immigration policy changed little. As turmoil and oppression of Jews and minority groups increased in Nazi Germany, refugees sought safety in the United States. But Congress failed to alter the visa limits created by the Johnson-Reed Act, so many refugees were turned away. The few who obtained visas were often met with hostility from their American neighbors, who were still reeling from the Great Depression and feared the newcomers would take their jobs.

In its first 170 years, the United States experienced mass immigration, broad immigration restrictions, and several waves of nativism as the country absorbed people with diverse beliefs, skills, and political ideas. Over the coming decades, immigration from new parts of the world would bring new opportunities and challenges to the United States.

ABOARD THE ST. LOUIS

In 1939, nearly 1,000 Jewish passengers boarded the German ocean liner *St. Louis* to flee persecution in Nazi Germany. The ship was bound for Havana, Cuba, where most passengers planned to stay temporarily before immigrating to the United States as refugees. Shortly before the ship sailed, Cuban president Federico Laredo Brú issued an order forbidding passengers from getting off the ship in Cuba. But the passengers of the *St. Louis* were not informed of this change. When the ship arrived in Havana on May 27, just 22 Jewish passengers with US visas were allowed off the ship. The remaining passengers, who were waiting for their visas to be processed, were to be sent back to Germany. Some passengers reached out to US President Franklin D. Roosevelt asking him to intervene, but the US public continued to support limits on immigration, even for refugees. The ship and most of its passengers sailed back to Europe, some of whom found refuge in other countries. By the end of World War II, nearly one-half of the passengers who remained stuck in Germany had perished in the Holocaust.[15]

CHAPTER THREE

AFTER
WORLD WAR II

World War II created history's largest population of displaced people. Millions of people fled their homes as their neighborhoods were battered by artillery and occupied by enemy forces. After the war ended, these families were living in refugee camps in Germany, Austria, and Italy. Many Jewish refugees immigrated to the new state of Israel. Other refugees sought to immigrate to the United States. Victorious in the war, the American people needed to decide whether it was in the national best interest to open the country's doors once again to mass immigration.

Belgian refugees fled a combat zone in 1945.

ADJUSTING TO POSTWAR NEEDS

In 1945, the Johnson-Reed Act was still in effect. It restricted immigration from many European countries regardless of a person's refugee status. But after witnessing the horrors of World War II, the American public and President Harry Truman decided it was time to adjust the country's immigration laws. President Truman issued an executive order called the Truman Directive in December 1945. It gave displaced people priority under the country's quota restrictions. As a result, nearly 23,000 displaced people immigrated to the United States by 1947.[1] In 1946, the annual number of immigrants entering the United States surpassed 100,000 for the first time in more than 15 years.[2]

In 1948, Congress passed the Displaced Persons Act. It expanded the Truman Directive to allow up to 200,000 people to enter the United States. By 1950, immigration to the United States reached 250,000.[3] The increase in quotas was not merely motivated by altruism. The Communist Soviet Union was a US ally in World War II. But tensions between the two counties had increased during the conflict, and they had become irreconcilable by the end of the war. The US government had growing concerns about the spread of communism domestically and abroad. Politicians argued that allowing more displaced persons into the United States meant fewer would immigrate to the Soviet Union and embrace communism.

IMMIGRANTS CROSS THE SOUTHERN BORDER

In the postwar years, the United States economy experienced an unprecedented boom. Entering the war in 1941 jump-started US manufacturing and brought the economy out of the Great Depression. The growth of the economy during the war continued once troops arrived home. Many Americans were making more money and improving their standard of living, and the promise of a

CROSSING THE BORDER

Many unauthorized immigrants enter the United States through the US-Mexico border. Doing so is no easy task, from surviving the hot, arid climate of the region to evading the tight security at the border itself. The smugglers paid to escort unauthorized immigrants across the border, called *coyotes*, are often untrustworthy. They steal migrants' money, attack them physically, and even abandon them in the desert. One notorious route through the Sonoran Desert of Arizona is called El Camino del Diablo, or "the Devil's Highway." More than 1,400 people have lost their lives navigating the old cattle and wagon trails that make up the route from Mexico into the United States.[4] Many die from heat exhaustion just miles from the nearest US town.

better life mobilized groups of people who had been historically denied their civil rights, including African Americans, Hispanics, and Asian Americans, to push for reform.

The strength of the US economy attracted people from countries near the United States that had not experienced a similar boom. During the war, the US government allowed immigration from Mexico under the *bracero* program. The program allowed Mexican citizens to work the fields in US farms. They took on difficult work under conditions many US citizens would not accept. The program was popular with US farmers, who enjoyed cheaper labor, and the program was renewed into the 1960s. But while the *bracero* program was in effect, another federal policy increased deportations of Mexicans, both legal and unauthorized immigrants. More than 4 million were deported to Mexico through the 1950s.[5]

In 1959, another group of refugees sought safety in the United States. That year, Fidel Castro and his supporters overthrew the Cuban government and established Communist rule on the island nation just 90 miles (145 km) south of Florida. In 1961, President John F. Kennedy created

Bracero workers picked chili peppers in California in 1964, supporting the US agricultural industry by accepting lower wages than US-born laborers.

the Cuban Refugee Program through executive order. Through the 1960s and early 1970s, approximately 600,000 Cuban refugees fled Cuba to settle in Miami, Florida, and elsewhere in the United States.[6]

A NEW IMMIGRATION SYSTEM

By the 1960s, the postwar increase in immigration required sweeping changes to modernize US immigration laws. In 1965, Congress passed the Hart-Celler Immigration Act. The act repealed the restrictive quota system established in the 1920s, as by 1965 the system was considered discriminatory against people from eastern and southern Europe. The act also made it easier for individuals to apply for visas for their families still living abroad. Without the quota system and with the new focus on reuniting families, the Hart-Celler Act led to an increase in immigration over the next few decades. In 1960, just 9.7 million immigrants lived in the United States, making up 5.4 percent of the total US population.[7] By 2015, 43.3 million immigrants lived in the United States, representing 13.5 percent of the population.[8]

Under the new system, annual immigration continued to grow. During the next 30 years, more than 18 million immigrants entered the US legally.[9] Meanwhile, conflicts abroad continued the need for the United States to welcome refugees. When the Vietnam War (1954–1975) ended, the United States prepared to receive approximately 130,000 Vietnamese refugees. Over the next few years, the number of people affected by the war and related conflicts in Cambodia and Laos increased the number of refugees from the region to 360,000.[10]

In the early 1980s, conflicts in El Salvador, Nicaragua, and other Central American countries forced many to flee their homes and seek refuge in the United States. Many of these people entered the country without securing the proper visa. By 1986, more than 3 million people lived in the United States without the required documentation. That year, Congress passed the Immigration Reform and Control Act. It increased border security while creating a path to legal residency for 2.7 million individuals who had arrived in the US illegally before 1982.[11] It also for the first time created a penalty for US businesses that knowingly hired unauthorized immigrants.

Despite these changes, legal and unauthorized immigration from Mexico and Central America continued to soar in the late 1980s and throughout the 1990s. Congress did not provide more money for border security, so illegal border crossings continued increasing. The law increased immigration enforcement and penalized businesses for hiring unauthorized immigrants. But it did not provide ways for businesses to hire more legal immigrants. Nor did it require businesses to thoroughly vet their workers'

"DURING THE NEXT 15 YEARS, ASSUMING A PERSISTENTLY STRONG ECONOMY, THE UNITED STATES WILL CREATE ABOUT 30 MILLION NEW JOBS. CAN WE AFFORD TO SET ASIDE MORE THAN 20 PERCENT OF THEM FOR FOREIGN WORKERS? NO. IT WOULD BE A DISSERVICE TO OUR OWN POOR AND UNFORTUNATE."[12]

—FATHER THEODORE M. HESBURGH, PRESIDENT OF NOTRE DAME UNIVERSITY AND CHAIRMAN OF THE SELECT COMMISSION ON IMMIGRATION AND REFUGEE POLICY OF CONGRESS, 1986 immigration statuses. Meanwhile, the need for labor did not decrease, leading to increased demand for cheap, though unauthorized, immigrant workers. By 1990, 3.5 million unauthorized immigrants lived in the United States. Reforms to the 1986 law in 1990 and 1996 bolstered border security and immigration law enforcement. But the population of unauthorized immigrants in the United States continued to grow, peaking in 2007 at 12.2 million.[13]

In 1996, Congress passed two pieces of immigration reform legislation. The Antiterrorism and Effective Death Penalty Act (AEDPA) was crafted in response to two terrorist attacks on the United States that occurred in 1993 and 1995. The law outlined the process for removing immigrants who were deemed terrorists by government intelligence agencies. It also restricted the immigration of people believed to be members of terrorist organizations. Together with the newly passed

THE IMMIGRATION ACT OF 1990

In 1990, Congress passed sweeping reform of the 1965 Hart-Celler Immigration Act and its subsequent amendments. The 1990 act created a worldwide cap on the number of visas available for family members of immigrants and for immigrants seeking employment in the United States. It also mandated that visas be awarded to countries underrepresented in the United States. No changes were made to the refugee program.

Illegal Immigration Reform and Immigrant Responsibility Act, AEDPA made it much more difficult for noncitizens to have the Supreme Court hear their deportation cases.

IMMIGRATION POST-SEPTEMBER 11

On September 11, 2001, terrorists hijacked commercial airliners and flew them into the World Trade Center towers in New York City and the Pentagon in Washington, DC. Passengers brought down another plane in a Pennsylvania field before it could reach its intended target. The attacks killed nearly 3,000 people.[14] The terrorists were members of the Islamist extremist group al-Qaeda. The attack prompted several changes that affected US immigration policy. A new government administration, the DHS, became responsible for managing the agencies that enforced the country's immigration policies. Spending on deportations and border enforcement increased, as did efforts to remove noncitizen criminals. Congress passed the 2001 Patriot Act and the 2005 REAL ID Act to help prevent potential terrorists from entering the country. It also began a system of registration for men and boys from predominantly Muslim countries called the National

Security Entry-Exit Registration System (NSEERS). Under NSEERS, noncitizen Muslim men and boys were required to report to an immigration office to be interviewed, photographed, and fingerprinted. This controversial program was shut down in 2011, but the regulation remained in place in case the government felt it were once again necessary. As a result of these immigration policy changes, immigration decreased dramatically for several years following the 9/11 attacks.

Meanwhile, famines and conflicts in Burma, the Middle East, and eastern Africa escalated, causing a crisis

Alabama was one of many states that updated its driver's licenses to comply with the 2005 REAL ID Act.

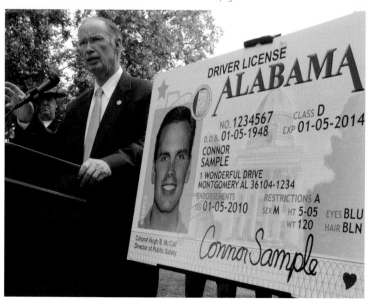

for people from countries such as Iran, Iraq, Somalia, and Sudan. The majority of people seeking refugee status from the Middle East and eastern Africa were Muslims. The new laws targeting potential terrorists made it more difficult for refugees from Muslim-majority countries to enter the United States. Despite these challenges, more than 50,000 refugees entered the United States in 2004, nearly double the number admitted in 2003. More than 13,000 of them were from Somalia alone, compared to just under 2,000 in 2003.[15] Since then, the annual number of refugees admitted to the United States has generally remained over the 50,000 mark.[16]

DRIVER'S LICENSES AND REAL ID

In recent years, some states and cities have allowed unauthorized immigrants to apply for identification cards. Under normal circumstances, unauthorized immigrants do not have the proper federal identification to apply for a state driver's license or ID card. But in 2017, 12 states and Washington, DC, allowed unauthorized immigrants to obtain driver's licenses after passing the required exams. Some cities have also enacted laws that allow unauthorized immigrants to obtain photo ID cards to use for identification purposes.

While unauthorized immigrants can use their driver's licenses in these 12 states to drive lawfully, these IDs do not comply with the federal REAL ID program. The REAL ID program requires state driver's license programs to confirm applicants' immigration statuses are compliant. If states fail to comply, all license holders in those states will eventually need another form of ID when going through airport security.

By the election of President Barack Obama in 2008, the post–September 11 immigration policy had been in place for nearly a decade. Under President Obama, annual deportations of unauthorized immigrants outpaced those under the last two administrations until 2013, when they began to decrease slightly. The Obama administration focused its deportation efforts along the country's borders and also targeted individuals who had committed crimes. During the same time, illegal border crossing dropped, a reversal of the trend over the last few decades. The president used executive orders to expand protections to certain unauthorized immigrants who had lived most of their lives in the United States.

"IF YOU MEET THE CRITERIA, YOU CAN COME OUT OF THE SHADOWS AND GET RIGHT WITH THE LAW. IF YOU'RE A CRIMINAL, YOU'LL BE DEPORTED. IF YOU PLAN TO ENTER THE US ILLEGALLY, YOUR CHANCES OF GETTING CAUGHT AND SENT BACK JUST WENT UP."[17]

—PRESIDENT OBAMA ON HIS EXECUTIVE ORDER TO REFORM IMMIGRATION, 2014

The complex history of immigration in the United States has touched every American community and people of every ethnicity. Today, the country continues to adjust its policies as newcomers continue to arrive seeking opportunity and freedom.

MORE TO THE
STORY

THE DREAMERS

The Deferred Action for Childhood Arrivals (DACA) order was announced in 2012. It allowed eligible unauthorized immigrants under the age of 31 who had been brought to the United States before their sixteenth birthdays to apply for a stay of deportation. If approved, DACA immigrants, called "Dreamers" in the media, could apply for work authorization and renew their DACA status every two years. The DACA order did not, however, give applicants legal status. A sister program, Deferred Action for Parents of Americans (DAPA), was announced in 2014 along with an expansion of DACA. DAPA extended similar protections to unauthorized immigrants who were parents of US citizens or lawful permanent residents who qualified.

The programs were immediately controversial because President Obama enacted them through executive orders rather than through Congressional legislation. A federal judge in Texas ordered a block of the DACA expansion and DAPA in 2015 on the grounds that the laws violated constitutional law. The case made it to the Supreme Court, which issued a 4-4 decision in 2016. The ruling meant that the Texas judge's block remained in effect, but the original DACA order stood. In September 2017, President Donald Trump's administration announced it would phase out DACA. The administration gave Congress six months to craft legislation to replace the order.

CHAPTER FOUR

IMMIGRATION
TODAY

If 2017 laws had been in place in the 1800s and early 1900s, many immigrants who were admitted would have been denied. It is no longer possible to lawfully immigrate to the United States without a visa. Visas require immigrants meet a specific set of criteria and are only given out in limited batches each year. There are rules for refugees and a specific process to follow to become a naturalized citizen.

KEY FEDERAL AGENCIES

Immigration law today is complex and requires dozens of federal, state, and local agencies to work together to

A US Customs and Border Protection agent checks people's passports as they arrive in the United States.

enforce it. The DHS manages several immigration agencies. USCIS receives visa petitions for new immigrants from US-based family members or businesses. ICE investigates reports of unauthorized immigration and manages the deportation of people who were staying unlawfully in the United States. Customs and Border Protection (CBP) guards the US border and checks paperwork at points of entry into the country.

The US Department of State manages embassies and consulates in other countries, from which the United States conducts diplomatic affairs. Citizens of foreign countries visit these offices to apply for immigrant visas and be personally interviewed. The National Visa Center handles Permanent Lawful Resident card (unofficially, green card) applications for USCIS. The Department of Labor verifies that employment visas have the proper certification.

DAY IN THE LIFE OF AN ICE AGENT

Agents serving in ICE are part of the DHS's largest investigative agency. Their top priority is to identify and remove immigrants who pose a threat to public safety or national security. On a typical day, an ICE agent may manage the intake of arrested immigrants at a detention center, facilitate medical exams for detained immigrants, and respond to phone calls from detainees and members of their families and communities.

INA GUIDING PRINCIPLES

The Immigration and Naturalization Act (INA) operates under four broad, guiding principles: reunite families, attract valuable skills, promote diversity, and protect refugees and asylees. To reunite families, priority goes to uniting US citizens or individuals in the United States who have green cards with their families abroad. The government approves more than 480,000 green cards for family members every year. Nearly two-thirds of all new lawful permanent residents in 2014 were family members of US citizens or lawful permanent residents already in the United States.[1] The foreign-born spouses, unmarried minor children, and parents of US citizens take first priority. They are followed by the adult

IMMIGRATION AGENCIES

Six federal agencies enforce national immigration law in the United States. The Department of Homeland Security oversees the work of USCIS, CBP, and ICE. The Department of State manages the Bureau of Population, Refugees, and Migration as well as the Bureau of Consular Affairs. The Department of Justice reviews and enforces immigration law, and the Department of Education oversees educational programs that support adult immigrants and school-age immigrant children. The Department of Health and Human Services manages the resettlement of refugees and creates policy around migrant worker health. Finally, the Department of Labor oversees agencies that regulate employment and job training for immigrants.

A legal permanent resident shows off her green card.

children and siblings of US citizens and the spouses and unmarried children of lawful permanent residents.

To attract valuable workers, immigrants with skills that are important to the US economy are given preference for green cards if they meet certain requirements. Approximately 140,000 employment-based permanent resident visas are available every year.[2] Most go to individuals with exceptional abilities, advanced degrees, and skilled work experience, along with their families. Employment-based green cards are available to immigrants who plan to invest money in a US business. There are more than 20 types of temporary work visas for nonimmigrant workers who wish to work in the United States for a limited time.

To promote diversity, the number of permanent immigrants from a particular country cannot represent more than 7 percent of the total number of permanent immigrants entering the United States in a single year. This policy ensures the United States does not favor a particular country or region for a long period of time. It also encourages emigration from countries or regions that are poorly represented in the United States. There is an annual limit of 55,000 for this type of green card that can be newly issued, and applicants must have a high school education or equivalent work experience.[3] In 2017, the diversity policy favored immigrants from Africa and eastern Europe. Diversity visas are available through a lottery system. Approximately 19 million people applied for 50,000 visas in 2017.[4]

The INA limits the number of lawful permanent residents admitted to the United States to approximately 675,000 a year. But to protect refugees and asylees, the president and Congress can set higher quotas for the number of refugees the country will accept above the INA limit. In 2016, the total limit for refugee visas was 85,000. Thirty-four thousand were allocated to the Near East and

South Asia, 25,000 to Africa, 13,000 to East Asia, and 4,000

to Europe and central Asia.[5]

The United States has a rigorous vetting system for

refugees. Those admitted are screened for the degree of

risk they face in their home countries. In addition, they

must prove they are members of a group about which

there is special concern, as defined by the president

or Congress. They receive preference if they have

family already residing the United States. Individuals

are screened by the DHS and Department of State to

determine whether they are

security risks, have criminal or

terrorist connections, or carry

a contagious disease. The

screenings include in-person

interviews and biometric

security checks. The entire

process, from application to

admission to the United States,

can take up to two years.

The INA also allows the

government to extend asylum

HOW CUSTOMS WORKS WITH OTHER NATIONS

The immigration law enforcement agencies within the DHS cooperate with agencies around the world. Together, they secure global trade networks, identify and apprehend international criminals and terrorists, and improve the safety and security of air travel. This cooperation also helps the United States provide emergency assistance in the event of a humanitarian crisis. The DHS employs personnel in more than 75 countries across the world to help protect the US border.

to people already in the United States. Asylees can seek protection based on persecution due to race, national origin, social group, political opinion, or religion. There is no limit to the number of individuals who can be granted asylum. Lastly, foreign-born individuals already in the United States who cannot return to their home countries due to a natural disaster or ongoing armed conflict may be granted temporary protected status for up to 18 months.

Historically, US refugee policy has often drawn controversy, such as turning away refugees fleeing Nazi Germany in the 1930s. The policy was a hotly debated topic in the 2016 election. The Syrian civil war began in 2011, and over the next several years, more than 5 million fled the country as refugees from the violence, half of them children.[6] Millions fled to neighboring countries and Europe. In time, the United States admitted Syrian refugees as they were vetted

"WITH SOME FOUR MILLION SYRIAN REFUGEES IN NEIGHBORING COUNTRIES AND HUNDREDS OF THOUSANDS OF SYRIAN ASYLUM SEEKERS IN EUROPE . . . WE URGE YOU TO TAKE EXTRAORDINARY MEASURES, AS WERE TAKEN FOR REFUGEES FROM VIETNAM, NORTHERN IRAQ, AND KOSOVO."[7]

—LETTER TO PRESIDENT OBAMA FROM FORMER SENIOR WHITE HOUSE OFFICIALS ON SYRIAN REFUGEES, 2015 through the US refugee system. In the year 2016, more than 12,500 Syrian refugees were admitted to the United States after completing the vetting program.[8] Given the volume of refugees, some felt this number was too low.

"WE CANNOT LET THEM INTO THIS COUNTRY, PERIOD. OUR COUNTRY HAS TREMENDOUS PROBLEMS. WE CAN'T HAVE ANOTHER PROBLEM."[9]

—DONALD TRUMP ON SYRIAN REFUGEES, 2015, DURING THE PRESIDENTIAL CAMPAIGN

But many political leaders and members of the public questioned the wisdom of allowing refugees from Syria—a majority-Muslim country—into the United States. In 2015, 30 governors declared they would not allow Syrian refugees to settle in their states, though federal law overruled any prohibition they set. During the 2016 presidential election, the majority of registered voters asserted the United States does not have the responsibility to accept Syrian refugees. People opposed to the refugees worried terrorists would make it through the vetting system and attack the United States, despite statistics showing that refugees almost never commit violent crimes.

Supporters hope President Trump's policies limiting immigration will make the country safer.

FROM THE HEADLINES

SYRIAN CIVIL WAR REFUGEES

The Syrian civil war began in 2011 between Syrian president Bashar al-Assad and anti-regime opposition, but it quickly evolved to also include forces from the Kurdish region of Iraq and the Islamic State (IS). By February 2013, 70,000 civilians had been killed in the conflict, and thousands had fled the fighting.[10] In August, anti-regime forces claimed Assad used chemical weapons against civilians, a claim later backed up by video and eyewitness accounts from physicians treating victims. Almost one year later, the United States launched air strikes against IS.

Meanwhile, millions of Syrians had fled their homes, the violence, and the attacks on citizens. Most Syrian refugees sought shelter in other Middle Eastern countries, including Turkey, Egypt, and Iraq. But more than 10 percent of all refugees migrated to Europe.[11] The influx of refugees put strain on many European nations, especially those in the Mediterranean who received refugees by boat from Turkey and North Africa. Thousands of refugees lost their lives making the treacherous journey due to overcrowded and flimsy boats and a lack of safety gear, food, and water.

Many Syrian refugees found shelter in camps in
the Middle East and Europe.

CHAPTER FIVE

IMMIGRATION AND
THE ECONOMY

Satya Nadella was born in Hyderabad, India, in 1967 to parents with professional careers. He studied at Manipal Institute of Technology in India before he secured a student visa to study in the United States. After studying computer science at the University of Wisconsin–Milwaukee, Nadella started interviewing for jobs. He had to find an employer who would work with him to obtain an employment visa. He was hired at Sun Microsystems in California. In 1992, he moved to Microsoft, where he was one of 30 Indian immigrant employees. In 2014, he became the company's CEO.

José lives in Orlando, Florida. He came to the United States when he was five years old. He lived a typical life

Many immigrants, including Satya Nadella of Microsoft, have made huge contributions to US businesses.

for a US kid, attending school and hanging out with his friends. When he was 15 years old, José learned he was an unauthorized immigrant. He had been brought to the United States without going through the visa process.

In 2017, José was 24 years old. Because he cannot prove he is a lawful resident, he could not purchase his first car, apply for college, or get a legitimate job.

Immigrants come to the United States from diverse backgrounds and for diverse reasons. Many come to the United States seeking better economic opportunities. For some, economic hardships in their home countries push them to immigrate to the country without applying for a visa, risking deportation. But most foreign-born workers in the United States have entered lawfully on an employment visa or temporary work visa.

"IT IS THE INGENUITY OF THE AMERICAN TECHNOLOGY THAT REACHED ME WHERE I WAS GROWING UP THAT EVEN MADE IT POSSIBLE FOR ME TO DREAM OF BEING ABLE TO BE PART OF THIS JOURNEY. IT IS THE ENLIGHTENED IMMIGRATION POLICY OF THIS COUNTRY THAT EVEN MADE IT POSSIBLE FOR ME TO COME HERE IN THE FIRST PLACE, AND GAVE ME ALL THIS OPPORTUNITY."[1]

—SATYA NADELLA, MICROSOFT CEO, 2017

IMMIGRATING ON AN EMPLOYMENT VISA

The United States offers hundreds of thousands of employment visas to foreign-born workers and their spouses and children every year—approximately 800,000 in 2015.[2] Employment visas, or E visas, are most likely to go to people with advanced skills or degrees. Generally, immigrants applying for an E visa must have a job lined up with an employer that is willing to sponsor the visa. The employer must also offer the job to US-born workers before the immigrant employee and have good reasons to reject US-born job applicants.

There are five pathways to obtaining a permanent E visa. The program prioritizes workers who are internationally renowned for their academic work, including professors and researchers. After this elite group, the program accepts applicants with advanced degrees or exceptional ability in their fields. Then the program accepts professional workers, skilled workers, and, lastly, unskilled workers. Another priority are religious workers and people planning to invest $1 million or more in a US business (or $500,000 in a business in a rural or economically depressed area).[3]

In addition to employment visas, which offer permanent residency to visa holders, the United States offers 11 types of temporary worker visas to foreign-born workers who wish to work in the United States for a fixed period of time. Like E visas, all temporary work visas require applicants to have an employer petition the government for the visa.

CONTRIBUTIONS TO THE US ECONOMY

Once immigrants arrive to work in the United States, they serve companies across a wide range of industries. As a group, immigrants are more likely than US-born workers to work in the service industry and the transportation, manufacturing, and materials-moving industries. They are also more likely to work in the construction and maintenance industries and the natural resources

"WHEN IMMIGRANTS ENTER THE LABOR FORCE, THEY INCREASE THE PRODUCTIVE CAPACITY OF THE ECONOMY AND RAISE GDP. THEIR INCOMES RISE, BUT SO DO THOSE OF NATIVES. IT'S A PHENOMENON DUBBED THE 'IMMIGRATION SURPLUS.'"[4]

—PIA ORRENIUS, THE BUSH CENTER, 2016

MORE TO THE
STORY

THE H-1B CONTROVERSY

An H-1B visa is one type of temporary worker visa. The H-1B visa program enables highly skilled, foreign-born workers to work for high-tech firms and research labs. When it was created in 1965, the program was intended to help US employers find skilled workers when none were available in the United States. Since then, the temporary visas—which allow workers to apply for permanent residence while they are employed—have become increasingly popular with tech firms. In 2016, nearly 570,000 workers applied for an H-1B, compared to just 100,900 in 2010.[5]

These visas have fallen under criticism from some politicians, who argue they allow companies to overlook potential US employees. In November 2016, President-Elect Trump announced he intended to investigate alleged abuse of the H-1B visa system and other temporary visas for evidence that they undermine US-born workers. Technology firms argue that without the visas, many technology jobs would go unfilled.

industry, including agricultural work. They are least likely

to serve in management, professional, or sales jobs.

Unauthorized immigrants in particular are more likely

to work in the service, construction, installation and

repair, transportation, and agricultural industries. Overall,

Mexican citizens line up at the US embassy in Mexico City, Mexico, hoping
to obtain temporary work visas to come to the United States.

unauthorized immigrant workers represent 5 percent of the entire US workforce but make up 26 percent of all farm workers and 15 percent of all construction workers.[6]

Foreign-born workers in the United States represented 17 percent of the American workforce in 2015, or approximately 27 million workers. Nearly one-half of this group is Hispanic, and nearly one-quarter is Asian.[7] Included in the total are approximately 8 million unauthorized workers, a number that has been relatively stable since 2009.[8] Immigrants are expected to make up an increasing percentage of the US workforce as US-born workers age and retire. New immigrants will be responsible for most of the growth of the US workforce. Without them, the number of workers in the United States would decline over time.

Every year, immigrants contribute to the US economy and pay taxes. Between 2009 and 2011, the wages, income, and revenue from immigrant-owned businesses generated 14.7 percent of the entire US economic output, even though immigrants represented just 13 percent of the entire US population.[9] Immigrant consumers also contribute billions of dollars per year to the economy.

UNAUTHORIZED-IMMIGRANT TAXES

Unauthorized immigrants pay nearly $12 billion per year in state and local income, property, sales, and excise taxes. The total amount varies from state to state, depending on the number of unauthorized immigrants residing there. In Montana, for example, unauthorized immigrants pay $2.2 million in state and local taxes. In California, which has a much larger unauthorized immigrant population, they contribute $3.2 billion.[10] In addition to state and local taxes, most unauthorized immigrants also contribute to the federal Social Security program through their paychecks, a program in which unauthorized immigrants cannot participate.

Both legal and unauthorized immigrants pay billions of dollars per year in property, sales, and federal, state, and local income taxes.

COSTS TO THE US ECONOMY

While immigrant workers contribute to the US economy, there are costs associated with both lawful and unauthorized immigration. Some Americans worry immigrant workers take jobs that should go to US-born workers. Others argue that immigrants fill many jobs US-born workers don't want.

Unauthorized immigrants do not receive welfare or other public assistance. Legal immigrants generally have to live in the country at least five years to qualify. However, all can attend public schools and receive emergency medical care. Citizen children of immigrants do qualify for benefits.

A study from the Heritage Center think tank estimates that an unauthorized immigrant household costs taxpayers $14,387 per year.[11] But most economists consider this an investment in the next generation's workforce.

Current US immigration policy offers immigrants who wish to work in the United States a pathway to do so. Still, some immigrants choose to seek work in the United States without going through the lawful channels. All immigrants together contribute billions of dollars each year to the US economy and are expected to become an increasingly large percentage of the US workforce. Economists, political leaders, and American workers often disagree about whether immigrant workers help or hinder the economic prospects of the nation and its native-born workers.

CHAPTER SIX

IMMIGRATION
AND THE LAW

I mmigrants have come to the United States seeking opportunity since the country was founded. And ever since, American people and their political leaders have debated who should be allowed into the country and how many immigrants should be allowed to enter. They also have argued over the effects immigrants have on US culture, the economy, and national security. This debate has shaped federal, state, and municipal immigration laws and policies for centuries, and it continues to do so today.

FEDERAL LAWS

Federal immigration law has gone through major changes over the last 200 years. Federal immigration

For many, the Statue of Liberty symbolizes the United States' openness to immigrants, even as immigration attitudes and laws shift over time.

law can change through three main avenues: congressional legislation, presidential executive order, and judicial action. Congress and the president work together to set annual limits on refugee admissions and determine any special groups the country will favor. Additionally, Congress can pass legislation to change current immigration laws or completely rewrite them. The Hart-Celler Act of 1965 was a wholesale change of US immigration policy that was amended over a number of decades before being overhauled in 1986 and again in 1990.

Presidents may shape immigration policy through executive order. Nearly every president since 1960 has taken executive action to direct immigration policy. Democratic president John F. Kennedy established a Cuban refugee program in 1961. Republican president Ronald Reagan protected the unauthorized children of parents who were legalized by the 1986 Immigration Reform and Control Act. In 2012, President Obama created the Deferred Action for Childhood Arrivals (DACA) program after the DREAM Act failed in Congress. DACA allows certain unauthorized immigrants who came to the

United States as children to apply for deferred action on being deported for a two-year period. Obama also expanded DACA by executive action in 2014.

Since executive orders create policy without the input of Congress, using them to direct immigration policy can backfire politically and constitutionally. One part of President Obama's executive order on DACA was blocked by the US Supreme Court in 2016. In this way, federal judges and federal courts also influence immigration policy.

THE DREAM ACT

The Development, Relief, and Education for Alien Minors Act, or DREAM Act, was introduced in Congress in 2009. It aimed to provide a pathway to legal status for high school graduates who came to the country illegally as children—an estimated 65,000 people per year. As the American Immigration Council notes, "These students are culturally American. . . . They tend to be bicultural and fluent in English. Many don't even know that they are undocumented immigrants until they apply for a driver's license or college."[1] The House of Representatives passed the bill in December 2010, but it died in the Senate. Forms of the DREAM Act have faced votes in Congress since 2001 but have always failed to pass despite bipartisan support. Some politicians have voted against the act because they want to vote on broader immigration reform instead. They worry passing the DREAM Act would stall other immigration legislation. Conversely, some politicians, especially Republicans, do not want to appear to support amnesty or forgiveness for unauthorized immigrants.

STATE AND LOCAL LAWS

While they must follow federal immigration law, states may also set immigration policy and law within their borders. State attorneys general may challenge federal laws in court. State legislatures may pass laws that limit how extensively state law enforcement departments and agencies cooperate with ICE. In Oregon, law enforcement agencies may not spend state tax dollars or resources to act as federal immigration officers if requested to do so by ICE. Several states have passed E-Verify requirements mandating that employers check every job applicant's legal status to identify unauthorized immigrants and prevent them from working in the United States. Other

Governor Jay Inslee of Washington, *center*, visits a center that provides cultural orientation for immigrants and helps them settle into their new lives.

states restrict social services for unauthorized immigrants.

Individual cities and towns may also pass rules and ordinances regarding immigration. As states do, municipalities may restrict their law enforcement agencies from enforcing federal immigration laws if asked to do so by ICE. Towns may offer or restrict social services, housing, and educational opportunities to immigrant families.

SERVICES FOR IMMIGRANTS

Federal, state, and local agencies provide social services to immigrants, refugees, and in some cases, temporary migrant workers. Federal programs help immigrant and refugee families adjust to life in the United States, overcome cultural and language barriers, and understand their rights as residents of the United States. Though they vary from place to place, state and local programs generally support federal efforts by providing child welfare support, food support, health care, and educational programs for immigrants, including classes for English as a second language.

STATE AND LOCAL PROTECTION FOR UNAUTHORIZED IMMIGRANTS

Two of the more controversial policies state and local governments have undertaken are the establishment of sanctuary cities and ID programs for unauthorized immigrants. Generally, sanctuary cities do not direct their law enforcement agencies to ask about or report the immigration statuses of people with whom police officers interact. Often, sanctuary cities also refuse to detain unauthorized immigrants for ICE after they have been arrested for low-level offenses such as petty theft. Though experts disagree on the exact number, there are an estimated 39 sanctuary cities and 364 sanctuary counties.[2]

While pro-immigration groups hail the efforts of sanctuary cities, others question the wisdom of protecting unauthorized immigrants from federal immigration laws. President Trump signed an executive order in January 2017 that threatened to cut federal funding for sanctuary cities. He said the cities violate federal law and put the safety of the American public at risk. However, Congress declined to defund sanctuary cities in its spring 2017 spending bill. In the same order, President Trump called for federal immigration agencies to expand their investigations and removal of unauthorized immigrants.

In most parts of the United States, federal, state, and municipal agencies work together to enforce immigration law and provide services to legal immigrants, unauthorized immigrants, and refugees. Deportations by ICE and border patrol officials generally rose between 2002 and 2014, with the most-dramatic increases targeting immigrants with a criminal conviction. However, the total number of deportations decreased in 2015, in part due to fewer people crossing the US-Mexico border. President Trump ran on the promise to continue to increase deportations. His promises focused on unauthorized immigrants and immigrants who have committed crimes or have ties to international crime or terrorism. The executive orders he signed in January 2017 called for increasing funding and hiring thousands more ICE agents to support the increase in deportation.

Lawmakers and political leaders will continue to shape immigration policy to reflect their own beliefs and those of their constituents. But many can be persuaded to change their positions, which is exactly what pro-immigration and anti-immigration groups, councils, and think tanks work to do.

"MANY ALIENS WHO ILLEGALLY ENTER THE UNITED STATES AND THOSE WHO OVERSTAY OR OTHERWISE VIOLATE THE TERMS OF THEIR VISAS PRESENT A SIGNIFICANT THREAT TO NATIONAL SECURITY AND PUBLIC SAFETY."[3]

—PRESIDENT DONALD TRUMP, EXECUTIVE ORDER: ENHANCING PUBLIC SAFETY IN THE INTERIOR OF THE UNITED STATES, 2017

FROM THE HEADLINES

THE TRAVEL BAN

On January 27, 2017, President Trump signed a sweeping travel ban into law through executive order. It created a 90-day ban on immigration from seven countries—Iran, Iraq, Libya, Somalia, Sudan, Syria, and Yemen—and an indefinite ban on Syrian refugees from entering the United States. The seven countries identified by the executive order were considered high terrorism risks, but critics noted the countries of origin of recent terrorists—Egypt, Lebanon, Saudi Arabia, and the United Arab Emirates—were left off the list. Immediately, reports spread of individuals and families being detained at airports across the country. Some were refugees, while others were students or permanent legal residents returning to school or home after trips abroad. Public protests erupted, and immigration attorneys set up temporary work spaces in baggage claims at several of the country's busiest international airports, including John F. Kennedy International Airport in New York City. The attorneys worked with family members of detained immigrants to understand the new law and argue for the immigrants' release.

One day later, Judge Ann M. Donnelly of the federal district court in Brooklyn, New York, issued a temporary block of the executive order. The ruling cited that sending the detained refugees and visa holders back to their countries of origin would cause them "irreparable harm."[4] A week after the judge's ruling, the Trump administration withdrew the entire executive order, replacing it with a revised order with the same name on March 6. The revised order removed Iraq from the list of banned countries and exempted permanent legal residents and visa holders from the law's provisions. It also set a limit on the previously indefinite ban on Syrian refugees to 120 days. Even with these exemptions and limitations, this second ban was also blocked by two judges as being unconstitutional on March 15. The administration issued a third travel ban on September 24.

In the confusion following the executive order, immigration attorneys offered free help at airports for people caught up in the ban.

CHAPTER SEVEN

THE CASE FOR
IMMIGRATION

Immigration has been part of the fabric of American culture and society since before the United States became a country. For centuries, people have immigrated to the United States to seek opportunity, safety, and freedom when their home countries could not provide them. And while every group of immigrants who have come to the United States has faced initial opposition from those already living in the United States, each group has contributed positively to the US economy, culture, and security.

IMMIGRATION AND THE ECONOMY

Pro-immigration experts often cite the need for more workers—both US- and foreign-born—to join the

Immigrants learn English and US politics in a US Department of Labor class in 1920.

workforce. This is especially true as people born between 1945 and 1964 retire. New immigrants can help turn around the falling pace of new businesses forming in the United States. Whether they work for a tech firm in Silicon Valley or build bridges in Oklahoma, immigrants increase both the supply of goods and the demand for them.

One point of disagreement between pro-immigration advocates and experts who recommend restricting immigration is the effect of lawful and unauthorized immigrants on the wages of US-born workers. Proponents of immigration cite research that over the long term, adding more low-skilled foreign-born workers to the US economy has very little effect on the wages of US-born workers. And over time, highly skilled immigrant workers have a positive impact on the wages of their US-born peers. Having these highly skilled immigrants in the area also benefits local workers who perform lower-skilled jobs in the service, transportation, and construction industries. Pro-immigration experts believe this is positive news for the future of the US economy as it evolves to include more highly skilled industries, such as information technology. However, limited-immigration proponents point to data that says immigrants drive down wages for low-skilled US-born workers.

IMMIGRATION AND US CULTURE

Every wave of immigrants to the United States has faced discrimination. Portions of the American public always fear that the newcomers will reject American values and cultural norms and in so doing, they will threaten the future of the United States. But immigration advocates point to historical and current examples that immigrant traditions strengthen and enrich American culture.

"IMMIGRATION IS NOT UNDERMINING THE AMERICAN EXPERIMENT; IT IS AN INTEGRAL PART OF IT."[1]

—DANIEL GRISWOLD, CATO INSTITUTE, 2002

Immigrants bring their skills, talents, and traditions to every aspect of American life, from how they worship and what they eat to the music they enjoy and the sports they play. These traditions become part of their American experience and eventually that of their US-born neighbors. Immigration advocates argue that these contributions are not only positive, they are part of what makes US culture exceptional.

Restaurants and food are some of the many ways immigrants have contributed to American culture.

IMMIGRATION AND NATIONAL SECURITY

Most people living in the United States agree that it is in the best interests of US-born and foreign-born residents alike to prevent dangerous people from entering the United States. There will always be people who wish to harm the United States who try to cross its borders. It is important for the country to protect its borders and its people. But experts disagree on whether strictly limiting immigration and cracking down on unauthorized immigrants are effective national security tactics for decreasing the threat of terrorism and other violence. Immigrants are not the only people from foreign countries who travel to the United States. Others are tourists, business travelers, and students. Daniel Griswold, former director of the conservative-leaning Cato Institute, points out that the 19 terrorists who carried out the September 11 attacks were allowed to enter the US on temporary visas for tourists and students, not as immigrants. Griswold argues that national security concerns would be better served by increasing investigations of foreign terrorist groups and their members.

CITIZENS TAKE ACTION

The United States has a long tradition of peaceful protest when Americans feel their voices are not being heard or their values are not being reflected in US immigration policy. Between March and May 2006, protests erupted across the country after Congress passed a law that restricted lawful immigration and increased enforcement for unauthorized immigrants. Millions of people marched in Chicago, Illinois; Los Angeles, California; and other US cities to protest the new law. Students in middle schools and high schools joined the protests, and on May 1, unauthorized immigrants across the country left work and school to boycott the law. A decade later, citizens also protested the immigration policies proposed by President Trump. When the first travel-ban executive order went into effect in late January 2017, spontaneous protests erupted at airports across the country where foreign-born people were being detained.

FINDING A SOLUTION FOR UNAUTHORIZED IMMIGRANTS

Immigration advocates and advocates for immigration restrictions agree that the country needs to act to reduce the number of unauthorized immigrants in the

VULNERABLE IMMIGRANTS EXPLOITED

New to the neighborhood, unfamiliar with US culture, and often lacking strong English skills, immigrants to the United States can fall victim to unscrupulous employers and landlords. The issue is worse for unauthorized immigrants, who often fear deportation if they report crimes to the police. Immigrants with little or no education and little knowledge of English are easy targets for human traffickers. Traffickers promise well-paying jobs and decent housing but instead force individuals into domestic service, farm labor, or prostitution for little or no pay. Often, traffickers steal immigrants' travel documents and identification to make escape difficult or impossible. ICE agents play a large role in investigating the exploitation of immigrants, prosecuting traffickers, and connecting victims with social services.

United States. But the two sides disagree on the best way to reduce unauthorized immigration. Generally, immigration advocates believe the best way to reduce the number of unauthorized immigrants in the United States is to offer unauthorized immigrants currently in the country a path to lawful residency. They also recommend expanding the visa program to encourage more people to enter the country lawfully in the first place. Nearly two-thirds of US adults support the idea of providing a path to citizenship for unauthorized immigrants living in the United States.[2] Doing the opposite—deporting all unauthorized immigrants and restricting lawful immigration—would be incredibly

Emergency responders make sure Cubans who arrived in Florida on a makeshift raft are recovering from their ordeal.

costly and nearly impossible logistically, according to pro-immigration experts.

Several national legal organizations advocate for immigrants' rights and work to influence immigration laws. The National Immigration Law Center defends the rights of low-income lawful and unauthorized immigrants through litigation and advocacy for pro-immigrant policy changes. The American Immigration Lawyers Association is a professional organization of immigration attorneys who represent immigrant families in the United States and US businesses that recruit foreign-born workers. The American Immigration Council challenges restrictive immigration laws in court and distributes information on immigration to the public.

The American Civil Liberties Union (ACLU) Immigrants' Rights Project uses public outreach, advocacy, and legal action. It works to ensure immigrants' civil rights are not violated by legislation or enforcement action its legal experts consider unconstitutional. ACLU legal observers are people trained to witness public demonstrations and law enforcement conduct for signs of legal misconduct. The National Immigrant Justice Center advocates for refugees, asylum seekers, and low-income immigrants, including children who immigrate to the United States without parents or guardians. Some national civil rights groups focus on advocating for the rights of certain minorities, including the National Council of La Raza for Latinos.

"THE FUNDAMENTAL CONSTITUTIONAL PROTECTIONS OF DUE PROCESS AND EQUAL PROTECTION EMBODIED IN OUR CONSTITUTION AND BILL OF RIGHTS APPLY TO EVERY PERSON, REGARDLESS OF IMMIGRATION STATUS."[3]

—AMERICAN CIVIL LIBERTIES UNION, 2017

Immigration advocates argue that immigrants not only contribute to, improve, and enrich the US economy and American culture, but they are also a vital part of what makes America stand out. Every US-born citizen, with the exception of Native Americans, has an ancestor who came to the United States from somewhere else. For immigration advocates, restricting legal immigration and cracking down on unauthorized immigration is not only harmful to the United States, it is un-American.

CHAPTER EIGHT

THE CASE
AGAINST
IMMIGRATION

Concern over the effects of immigration on the US economy, culture, and security has been a fixture of American society since the country's founding. US-born workers and political leaders have long worried that low-cost immigrant labor takes the jobs and wages earned by US citizens. Communities have felt concern about how well their new neighbors would adjust to American life because they spoke different languages, ate unfamiliar foods, and worshipped differently. And some leaders in politics and law

Many immigrants work as day laborers, looking for short-term projects such as gardening, construction, or cleaning.

enforcement warn that allowing so many foreign people to move to the United States leaves the country vulnerable to terrorism and other violence.

IMMIGRATION AND THE ECONOMY

On average, households headed by an immigrant worker make $681 a week. This is lower than the $837 of the average US-born households.[1] While in 2015, 66 percent of immigrants were in the workforce, 16.5 percent of these lived in poverty and 22 percent lacked health insurance.[2] In comparison, the US poverty rate overall that year was 13.5 percent.[3] Although unauthorized immigrants cannot receive federal benefits directly and authorized immigrants do not qualify immediately, US-born children of these immigrants do receive benefits. Experts who advocate for restricting immigration and deporting unauthorized immigrants rather than creating a pathway to citizenship argue that such immigrant-headed households living in poverty are a drain on the US economy. According to a National Academies of Sciences study, each adult immigrant in the United States cost his or

MORE TO THE STORY

THE 2016 ELECTION

"When Mexico sends its people, they're not sending their best," asserted Donald Trump when he announced his candidacy in June 2015. "They're sending people that have lots of problems, and they're bringing those problems with us."[4] Over the next 18 months, immigration would become a talking point of presidential hopefuls on both sides of the aisle. In the spring of 2015, more than 60 percent of Republican voters believed that immigration harmed the United States more than it strengthened it.[5] If elected, Republican nominee Trump promised to build a border wall that reached across the entire US-Mexico border, deport all unauthorized immigrants, remove funding for sanctuary cities, limit lawful immigration, and suspend immigration from terror-prone regions.

Immigration was a talking point of Democratic nominee Hillary Clinton, too. Although more than 60 percent of Republicans believed immigration was a net burden, a nearly equal number of Democrats believed the opposite—that immigration strengthened the United States.[6] If elected, Clinton vowed she would propose a path to citizenship for unauthorized immigration, continue to support DACA, deport violent criminals, and rely on technology and more border patrol agents to secure the US-Mexico border.

her state and local governments $1,600 combined over the period from 2011 to 2013.[7]

According to the National Academies of Sciences study, immigration has positive effects on some aspects of the US economy but other negative effects. Low-wage immigrant labor is good for the businesses that save money. But the study also finds that immigration can drive down wages for everyone, so low-skill US-born workers lose money.

On average, immigrants have slightly less education than their US-born peers. In 2015, approximately 29 percent of immigrants over age 25 had college degrees, similar to the 31 percent of native-born Americans who have attained that level of education. However, while only 9 percent of native-born Americans do not have a high school education, 29 percent of immigrants lack this credential. Approximately half of immigrants older than five years were not able to speak English.[8]

IMMIGRATION AND US CULTURE

A persistent concern of many Americans and limited-immigration advocates is the influence immigrants

will have on American culture and quality of life.
Accommodating the employment, housing, health care,
educational, and religious needs of individuals and families
who may have limited educations and English-language
skills is an enormous challenge. It requires effort and
funding that could instead support US citizens and the
US economy.

Some experts who oppose immigration are concerned
that the millions of immigrants in the United States will
change American culture instead of assimilating into it.
Nowhere is the effect of immigration on American society
more clear than in the country's schools. Experts project
that by 2035 more than one-third of schoolchildren
will be immigrants or the
children of immigrants.[9]
The large immigrant and
second-generation populations
in some public schools can
make it difficult for students
to assimilate to American
culture. Conservative
groups point to the extra

"ALREADY ONE IN FOUR
OKLAHOMA CHILDREN
STRUGGLE(S) WITH HUNGER. ONE
IN FOUR WILL DROP OUT OF HIGH
SCHOOL BEFORE GRADUATING. IT
IS WRONG FOR THE PRESIDENT
TO ASK OKLAHOMANS TO DIVERT
THEIR ATTENTION AND LIMITED
RESOURCES AWAY FROM OUR
OWN CHILDREN."[10]

—OKLAHOMA GOVERNOR
MARY FALLIN

costs immigrant children can cause schools, including needing additional English instruction or other support. Public schools are required by US law to accept all students, regardless of whether they or their parents are unauthorized immigrants.

IMMIGRATION AND NATIONAL SECURITY

Throughout US history, Americans have been concerned that some of the immigrants who enter the country, either lawfully or without authorization, have bad intentions. In 2015, 333,000 immigrants were deported. Of these, 42 percent had been convicted of a crime.[11] Limited-immigration advocates believe enforcing immigration law and prioritizing the removal of criminal immigrants would help make the country safer.

The threat of terrorism at the hands of immigrants and refugees is another concern. The outbreak of the Syrian civil war in 2011 caused an influx of millions of displaced Syrians into Europe. An uptick in terrorist acts in Europe accompanied

"IT IS OUR RIGHT AS A SOVEREIGN NATION TO CHOOSE IMMIGRANTS THAT WE THINK ARE THE LIKELIEST TO THRIVE AND FLOURISH AND LOVE US."[12]

—DONALD TRUMP, SEPTEMBER 2016

Arizona residents rally to support stronger immigration laws passed in the state in 2010.

the wave of migrants as Islamic State fighters infiltrated European cities along the same routes as families seeking safety. In the United States, many law enforcement experts and members of the public fear that admitting Syrian refugees could expose the United States to similar attacks, despite a rigorous refugee vetting system. In early 2017, President Trump twice tried to ban Syrian refugees from entering the United States. Both attempts were blocked temporarily by federal judges, but parts of the travel ban went into effect in June. A third travel ban, issued on September 24, changed the list of countries under scrutiny. The restrictions vary for the eight countries on the list, and the overall effect on refugees was unclear in the administration's announcement.

FINDING A SOLUTION FOR UNAUTHORIZED IMMIGRANTS

PATROLLING THE BORDER

The US border patrol base in Douglas, Arizona, received the call from a desperate migrant. The man frantically told the border patrol agent who took the call that his sister-in-law was in the desert suffering from heat exhaustion. A search team was sent out to rescue the woman, who was attempting to cross the border illegally. An hour later, the news came in over the radio: a search team had found the woman, but she had perished in the heat. Often, agents arrive in time to save lives; other times, they are too late. Rescuing wayward and exhausted migrants is just one part of a border patrol agent's role. Agents are responsible for preventing unauthorized immigrants, criminals, and drugs from entering the country. The job requires investigation skills, state-of-the-art technology, and a lot of legwork. Like the migrants they track, many border patrol agents spend their days and nights in the desert, navigating rough terrain and coping with the dry desert heat.

For people who support reducing immigration, enforcing current law that requires unauthorized immigrants to be deported is a top priority. In his early presidency, President Trump continued to push for building a wall along the border with Mexico. A border wall, though expensive, could prevent some unauthorized immigrants from entering the United States. However, many immigrants become unauthorized by entering the country lawfully but overstaying their visas. Increased enforcement of current immigration laws and enhanced employment verification systems would further deter and decrease unauthorized immigration.

Several national groups work to reduce or eliminate unauthorized immigration, reduce the number of immigrants entering the United States, or support the agencies enforcing current immigration law. The Federation for American Immigration Reform is a nonpartisan group that advocates for laws that reduce both lawful and unauthorized immigration and prioritize the political and economic interests of American citizens. The Midwest Coalition to Reduce Immigration is a volunteer group that promotes reducing immigration levels to protect American jobs and preserve the environment against overpopulation.

Advocates of reducing immigration argue that lawmakers must craft federal, state, and local immigration policies that put the strength of the US economy and protection of US workers, culture, and safety ahead of other concerns. According to limited-immigration advocates, participating in America's rich traditions of opportunity, safety, and freedom for all citizens is a privilege, not a right, for foreign-born individuals.

CHAPTER NINE

LOOKING
AHEAD

Experts predict that by 2065 more than one-third of the people living in the United States will be immigrants or children of immigrants, up from one-quarter in 2015.[1] Immigrants will be the main driver of population growth in the United States. Without this influx of new immigrants and their children, the US population is projected to stagnate as older generations pass away and the birth rate among younger generations decreases.

Immigrants from Asia will be the source of the greatest increase. Asian immigrants, who represented 26 percent of immigrants in 2015, will represent 38 percent of all immigrants by 2065. Because Asian immigrants tend to be more educated than other

A significant and growing number of US residents are immigrants.

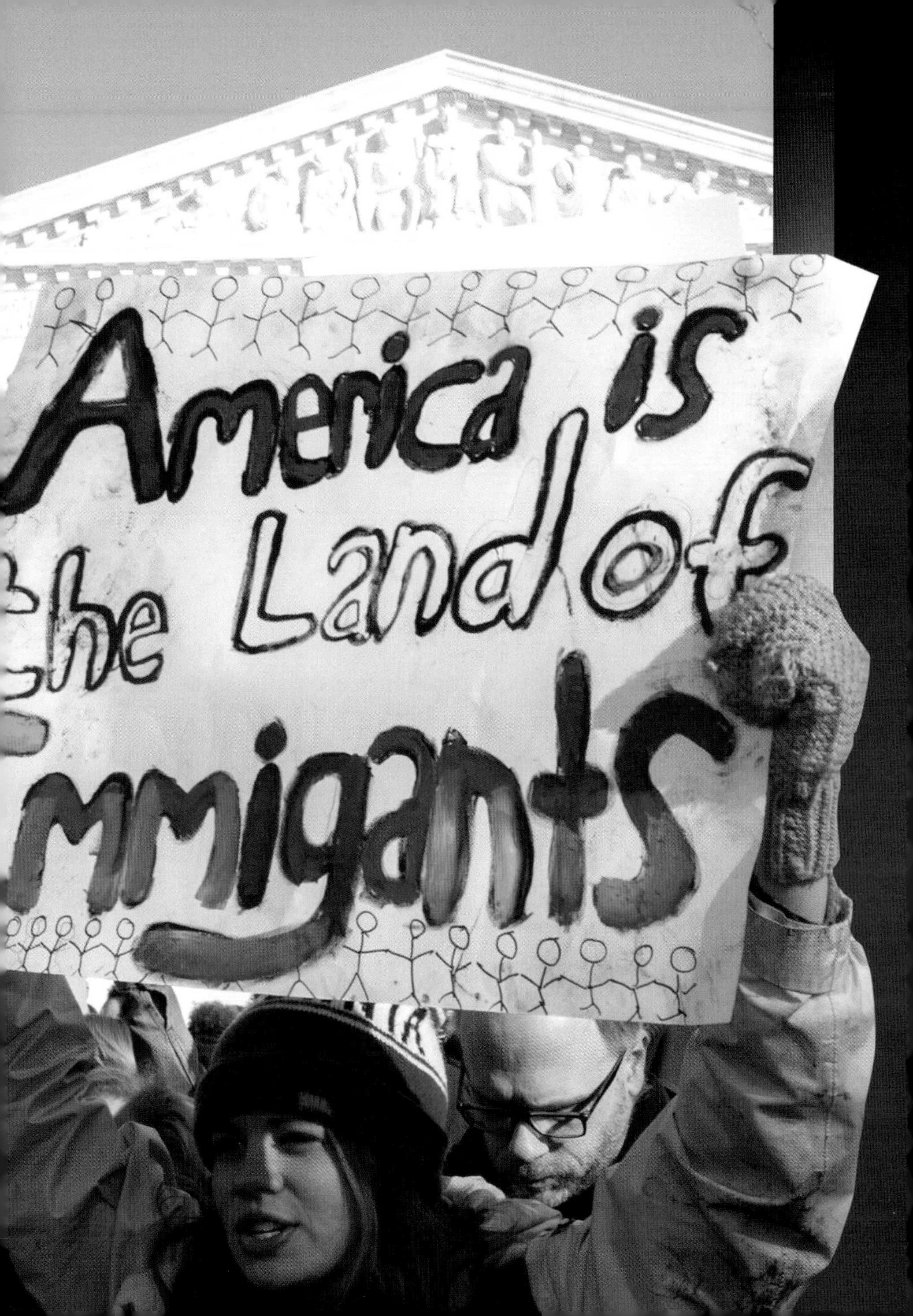
America is
Land of

immigrant groups, their presence in the United States may increase the number of highly skilled workers in the country overall. Meanwhile, the percentage of immigrants from Mexico will decrease from 47 percent to 31 percent by 2065, and no racial or ethnic group will have a majority.[2]

CLIMATE CHANGE AND IMMIGRATION

Immigrants have long migrated to the United States to flee economic, political, and religious oppression. But experts predict another crisis will increase immigration in the future: climate change. Scientists predict rising global temperatures will cause an increase in droughts in Central America, which will cause a fall in crop production and strain resources in the region. Millions of out-of-work agricultural workers and hungry people could migrate north to the United States. Scientists urge political leaders to consider climate change when developing new immigration policies.

PRESIDENT TRUMP'S ACTION ON IMMIGRATION

These predictions are based on current immigration laws. But these policies may change over the next few decades. President Trump campaigned on massive overhauls to the US immigration system. In his first 100 days in office, he signed several executive orders that could affect immigration. One executive order threatened to pull federal funding from sanctuary cities unless they would comply with federal immigration law. Another called for increased funding for

US government plans in 2017 called for increasing border patrols.

ICE and other law enforcement to combat international organized crime and apprehend criminal immigrants. And another executive order directed the government to start planning a wall along the US-Mexico border, as well as increase deportations of all unauthorized immigrants.

On the campaign trail, President Trump opposed providing a pathway to citizenship for unauthorized immigrants. He preferred requiring unauthorized immigrants to return to their home countries and apply for visas or risk deportation. But some immigration experts have proposed plans that allow unauthorized immigrants to apply for lawful permanent residency. These experts assert that an effective legalization program will need to strike a balance between family reunification, fair but meaningful penalties, and treating otherwise law-abiding individuals humanely. A program must be simple, with a low barrier to participation to protect against deportation and increase the likelihood that unauthorized immigrants will take advantage of the program.

OTHER REFORMS

Border walls, increased enforcement, and paths to legalization for unauthorized immigrants are just some proposed ways to improve the US immigration system. Economists, public policy experts, and political leaders have a wide range of other

Cars line up to cross the border at every US point of entry, including San Ysidro, California.

ideas, too. Experts at the Economic Policy Institute recommend tying the number of employment-based visas available in any given year to the US labor market. Currently, the government sets annual visa limits that do not adapt to the strength of the US economy. Under the proposed system, the government could increase the number of visas available when the economy is strong and unemployment is low. It could decrease the number available in weak years when unemployment is high. This would reduce the number of foreign workers competing with US-born workers for jobs.

Other ideas offer ways to recruit immigrants who will contribute positively to the US economy and culture. Pascal-Emmanuel Gobry, a fellow at the Ethics and Public Policy Center, suggested in 2013 that the United States shift its policy focus from keeping out undesirable immigrants to recruiting immigrants with skills and characteristics that embody American values. Gobry also suggests opening up the US Marine Corps to foreigners who are not yet immigrants. They would commit to serving in the US military and learning English in exchange for becoming lawful permanent residents of the United States. Other experts recommend creating a visa lottery system in which employers pay a fee to participate in a drawing to sponsor foreign workers. The new system would also eliminate quotas for immigration from certain countries and prioritize uniting spouses, parents, and children before extended family members.

Policies, laws, and public attitudes will shape the future of the American immigration system. But individuals and families will continue to move to the United States seeking more opportunity, freedom, and safety. The challenge of creating a fair and effective US immigration system has always been balancing the best interests of the US economy and American people with the hopes, ambitions, and basic human rights of people outside the country's borders.

Immigrant children take the oath of citizenship in New York in 2017.

ESSENTIAL
FACTS

MAJOR EVENTS

- Congress passes the country's first restriction on immigration, the Chinese Exclusion Act, in 1882.

- On March 3, 1891, Congress passes the Immigration Act of 1891, federalizing the US immigration system.

- The Hart-Celler Immigration Act of 1965 overhauls the US immigration system.

- The terrorist attacks of September 11, 2001, prompt several reforms to immigration to stop terrorists from entering the country, including the REAL ID Act and NSEERS.

- In his first 100 days in office, President Donald Trump signs a number of executive orders pertaining to immigration.

KEY PLAYERS

- Highly skilled and low-skilled workers, refugees, and family members of earlier immigrants make up most of the new immigrants to the United States.

- The US Congress is responsible for crafting and updating federal immigration laws, but the US president can sign executive orders to make immigration policy, too. Federal judges interpret these laws. State and local municipalities also pass laws and ordinances regarding the treatment of immigrants by law enforcement.

- Executing and enforcing immigration law involves many federal, state, and local agencies, including US Citizenship and Immigration Services, US Immigration and Customs Enforcement, and US Customs and Border Protection, while several national organizations advocate for expanding or restricting immigration and for the civil rights of immigrants.

IMPACT ON SOCIETY

Regardless of national origin, immigrants bring new and different languages, skills, religions, and cultures to the United States. Working-age immigrants are predicted to make up a large portion of the American workforce as US-born workers retire. Unauthorized immigration continues to be a concern for most Americans, but the public disagrees on the best way to address the issue.

QUOTE

"The Bosom of America is open to receive not only the Opulent and respectable Stranger, but the oppressed and persecuted of all Nations and Religions."

—President George Washington

GLOSSARY

ANARCHIST
Having to do with the belief that countries should not have governments.

ASSIMILATE
To adopt the ways of another culture.

BIOMETRIC
Relating to the analysis of physical characteristics such as fingerprints or voice patterns.

BIPARTISAN
Involving both political parties.

COMMODITY

Something that has value and is bought and sold.

COMMUNIST

Having to do with a system in which the government controls the economy and owns all property.

EXCISE TAX

A tax charged on the purchase of a specific product.

JUDICIAL

Relating to the function of the court system.

MIGRANT WORKER

A person who moves from place to place to do seasonal work.

NATIVISM

An attitude or policy of favoring native people over immigrants.

NATURALIZED

Given the rights of citizenship.

ADDITIONAL
RESOURCES

SELECTED BIBLIOGRAPHY

Bray, Ilona. *US Immigration Made Easy*. 18th Ed. Berkeley, CA: Nolo, 2017. Print.

"Citizenship Rights and Responsibilities." *Citizenship Resource Center*. US Citizenship and Immigration Services, n.d. Web. 5 July 2017.

"US Visas." *US Department of State*. US Department of Homeland Security, n.d. Web. 5 July 2017.

FURTHER READINGS

Hauser, Brooke. *The New Kids: Big Dreams and Brave Journeys at a High School for Immigrant Teens*. New York: Free, 2011. Print.

Rowell, Rebecca. *William Williams Documents Ellis Island Immigrants*. Minneapolis: Abdo, 2018. Print.

St. John, Warren. *Outcasts United: The Story of a Refugee Soccer Team That Changed a Town*. New York: Delacorte, 2012. Print.

ONLINE RESOURCES

Booklinks
NONFICTION NETWORK
FREE! ONLINE NONFICTION RESOURCES

To learn more about US immigration policy, visit **abdobooklinks.com**. These links are routinely monitored and updated to provide the most current information available.

MORE INFORMATION

For more information on this subject, contact or visit the following organizations:

Ellis Island Museum of Immigration
Statue of Liberty National Monument
New York, NY 10004
212-363-3200
nps.gov/elis/index.htm
Visit Ellis Island, where millions of immigrants first set foot on US soil.
Visit the Baggage Room, where immigrants stored their belongings during
the admittance process, and the Registry Room, where new arrivals
waited to be registered and inspected. Learn all about the immigrants
who passed through the island or do some family history research.

National Border Patrol Museum
4315 Woodrow Bean Transmountain Road
El Paso, TX 79924
915-759-6060
borderpatrolmuseum.com
Learn all about border patrol operations throughout history while taking
a look at the equipment border patrol agents have used to protect
the US border. Sit in a border patrol helicopter and discover how border
checkpoints have changed over time.

SOURCE
NOTES

CHAPTER 1. DANGEROUS WORK REWARDED

1. "No One Left Behind." *No One Left Behind.* No One Left Behind, n.d. Web. 5 July 2017.

2. Kavitha Surana. "Special Visas for Afghan Interpreters Are Running Out." *Cable.* Foreign Policy, 10 Mar. 2017. Web. 5 July 2017.

3. Ibid.

4. Blair Miller. "Afghan Translator Now in Denver Vetted for 2 Years before Special Visa Was Approved." *Denver Channel.* Scripps TV Station Group, 1 Feb. 2017. Web. 5 July 2017.

5. Gustavo López and Kristen Bialik. "Key Findings About U.S. Immigrants." *Fact Tank.* Pew Research Center, 3 May 2017. Web. 5 July 2017.

6. Jie Zong and Jeanne Batalova. "Frequently Requested Statistics on Immigrants and Immigration in the United States." *Migration Information Source.* Migration Policy Institute, 8 Mar. 2017. Web. 5 July 2017.

CHAPTER 2. "YOUR TIRED, YOUR POOR"

1. Dennis Wepman. *Immigration: From the Founding of Virginia to the Closing of Ellis Island.* New York: Facts on File, 2002. Print. 192.

2. Ibid. 35.

3. Ibid. 41.

4. "From George Washington to Joshua Holmes, 2 December 1783." *Founders Online.* National Archives, 29 June 2017. Web. 5 July 2017.

5. Dennis Wepman. *Immigration: From the Founding of Virginia to the Closing of Ellis Island.* New York: Facts on File, 2002. Print. 80.

6. "Facts about the Slave Trade and Slavery." *History by Era.* Gilder Lehrman Institute of American History, 2017. Web. 5 July 2017.

7. "From Indentured Servitude to Racial Slavery." *Africans in America.* PBS, 1999. Web. 5 July 2017.

8. Dennis Wepman. *Immigration: From the Founding of Virginia to the Closing of Ellis Island.* New York: Facts on File, 2002. Print. 363.

9. Ibid. 206.

10. Ibid. 210.

11. "Republican Party Platform of 1864." *Political Party Platforms.* American Presidency Project, 2017. Web. 5 July 2017.

12. "The New Colossus—Full Text." *National Park Service.* US Department of the Interior, 15 Nov. 2016. Web. 5 July 2017.

13. Dennis Wepman. *Immigration: From the Founding of Virginia to the Closing of Ellis Island.* New York: Facts on File, 2002. Print. 363.

14. United States Congress. *Congressional Record: Proceedings and Debates of the Third Session of the Sixty-Sixth Congress of the United States of America Volume LX – Part 1.* Washington, DC: US Government Printing Office, 1921. *Google Book Search.* Web. 5 July 2017.

15. "Voyage of the *St. Louis.*" *Holocaust Encyclopedia.* United States Holocaust Memorial Museum, n.d. Web. 5 July 2017.

CHAPTER 3. AFTER WORLD WAR II

1. "New Directive on Immigrant Visas to the US." *Timeline of Events.* United States Holocaust Memorial Museum, n.d. Web. 5 July 2017.

2. David W. Haines. "Learning from Our Past: The Refugee Experience in the United States." *Research.* American Immigration Council, 25 Nov. 2015. Web. 5 July 2017.

3. Lewis Siegelbaum. "Cold War." *Seventeen Moments in Soviet History.* Michigan State University, n.d. Web. 5 July 2017.

4. ABC News. "One Night on a Deadly Border Crossing." *ABC News.* ABC, 8 Aug. 2017. Web. 5 July 2017.

5. "Mexican." *Immigration.* Library of Congress, n.d. Web. 5 July 2017.

6. "Castro Announces Mariel Boatlift." *This Day in History: April 20.* A&E Television Networks, 2017. Web. 5 July 2017.

7. Gustavo López and Jynnah Radford. "Statistical Portrait of the Foreign-Born Population in the United States." *Hispanic Trends.* Pew Research Center, 3 May 2017. Web. 5 July 2017.

8. Jie Zong and Jeanne Batalova. "Frequently Requested Statistics on Immigrants and Immigration in the United States." *Migration Information Source.* Migration Policy Institute, 8 Mar. 2017. Web. 5 July 2017.

9. "U.S. Immigration Since 1965." *History.com.* A&E Television Networks, n.d. Web. 5 July 2017.

10. Drew DeSilver. "Executive Actions on Immigration Have Long History." *Fact Tank.* Pew Research Center, 21 Nov. 2014. Web. 5 July 2017.

11. Brad Plumer. "Congress Tried to Fix Immigration Back in 1986. Why Did It Fail?" *Wonkblog.* Washington Post, 30 Jan. 2013. Web. 5 July 2017.

12. Theodore M. Hesburgh. "Enough Delay on Immigration." *New York Times.* New York Times, 20 Mar. 1986. *Expanded Academic ASAP.* Web. 5 July 2017.

13. "Unauthorized Immigrant Population Trends for States, Birth Countries and Regions." *Hispanic Trends.* Pew Research Center, 3 Nov. 2016. Web. 5 July 2017.

14. "Facts about 9/11." *Teach + Learn.* National September 11 Memorial & Museum, 2017. Web. 5 July 2017.

15. Nancy F. Rytina. "Refugee Applicants and Admissions to the United States: 2004." *Office of Immigration Statistics.* US Department of Homeland Security, Sept. 2005. Web. 5 July 2017.

16. Ruth Igielnik and Jens Manuel Krogstad. "Where Refugees to the US Come From." *Fact Tank.* Pew Research Center, 3 Feb. 2017. Web. 5 July 2017.

17. Jim Acosta and Stephen Collinson. "Obama: 'You Can Come Out of the Shadows.'" *CNN: Politics.* Turner Broadcasting System, 21 Nov. 2014. Web. 5 July 2017.

CHAPTER 4. IMMIGRATION TODAY

1. "How the United States Immigration System Works." *American Immigration Council.* American Immigration Council, 12 Aug. 2016. Web. 5 July 2017.

2. Ibid.

3. Ibid.

4. Phillip Conner. "Applications for U.S. Visa Lottery More Than Doubled Since 2007." *Fact Tank.* Pew Research Center, 24 Mar. 2017. Web. 5 July 2017.

5. "How the United States Immigration System Works." *American Immigration Council.* American Immigration Council, 12 Aug. 2016. Web. 5 July 2017.

6. World Vision Staff. "Syrian Refugee Crisis: Facts You Need to Know." *Refugees.* World Vision, 13 Apr. 2017. Web. 5 July 2017.

SOURCE NOTES
CONTINUED

7. Michael R Gordon. "Ex-Officials Urge White House to Accept More Syrian Refugees." *New York Times*. New York Times, 17 Sept. 2015. Web. 5 July 2017.

8. Jens Manuel Krogstad and Jynnah Radford. "Key Facts about Refugees to the US." *Fact Tank*. Pew Research Center, 30 Jan. 2017. Web. 5 July 2017.

9. Tal Kopan. "Donald Trump: Syrian Refugees a 'Trojan Horse'." *CNN: Politics*. Turner Broadcasting System, 16 Nov. 2015. Web. 5 July 2017.

10. Associated Press. "Timeline: How the U.S. Has Responded to Syria's Civil War." *PBS NewsHour: The Rundown*. NewsHour Productions, 6 Apr. 2017. Web. 5 July 2017.

11. World Vision Staff. "Syrian Refugee Crisis: Facts You Need to Know." *Refugees*. World Vision, 13 Apr. 2017. Web. 5 July 2017.

CHAPTER 5. IMMIGRATION AND THE ECONOMY

1. Microsoft Corporate Blogs. "Response to the Jan. 27 US Executive Order on Immigration." *Microsoft on the Issues*. Microsoft Corporation, 31 Jan. 2017. Web. 5 July 2017.

2. "Employment-Based Visa Categories in the United States." *American Immigration Council*. American Immigration Council, 13 Sept. 2016. Web. 5 July 2017.

3. Ilona Bray. *US Immigration Made Easy*. 18th Ed. Berkeley, CA: Nolo, 2017. Print. 262.

4. Pia Orrenius. "Benefits of Immigration Outweigh the Costs." *Catalyst*. George W. Bush Presidential Center, Spring 2016. Web. 5 July 2017.

5. "Why H-1B Visas Are So Controversial." *Washington Post*. Washington Post, 6 Feb. 2017. Web. 5 July 2017.

6. Jens Manuel Krogstad, Jeffery S. Passel, and D'Vera Cohn. "5 Facts about Illegal Immigration in the U.S." *Fact Tank*. Pew Research Center, 27 Apr. 2017. Web. 5 July 2017.

7. "Foreign-Born Workers: Labor Force Characteristics–2016." *News Release Bureau of Labor Statistics*. US Department of Labor, 18 May 2017. Web. 5 July 2017.

8. Jens Manuel Krogstad, Jeffery S. Passel, and D'Vera Cohn. "5 Facts about Illegal Immigration in the U.S." *Fact Tank*. Pew Research Center, 27 Apr. 2017. Web. 5 July 2017.

9. Daniel Costa, David Cooper, and Heidi Shierholz. "Facts About Immigration and the U.S. Economy." *EPI FAQ*. Economic Policy Institute, 12 Aug. 2014. Web. 5 July 2017.

10. Andrew Soergel. "'Undocumented' Immigrants Pay Billions in Taxes." *US News and World Report*. US News and World Report, 1 Mar. 2016. Web. 5 July 2017.

11. Maria Santana. "5 Immigration Myths Debunked." *CNN Money*. Cable News Network, 20 Nov. 2014. Web. 5 July 2017.

CHAPTER 6. IMMIGRATION AND THE LAW

1. "The DREAM Act." *American Immigration Council.* American Immigration Council, 13 July 2010. Web. 5 July 2017.

2. Jessica Tarlton and Matthew Green. "What Are Sanctuary Cities and How Are They Bracing for Trump's Immigration Crackdown? (with Lesson Plan)." *The Lowdown.* KQED, 7 Feb. 2017. Web. 5 July 2017.

3. Donald J. Trump. "Executive Order: Enhancing Public Safety in the Interior of the United States." *The White House.* The White House, 25 Jan. 2017. Web. 5 July 2017.

4. Michael D. Shear, Nicholas Kulish, and Alan Feuer. "Judge Blocks Trump Order on Refugees Amid Chaos and Outcry Worldwide." *New York Times.* New York Times, 28 Jan. 2017. Web. 5 July 2017.

CHAPTER 7. THE CASE FOR IMMIGRATION

1. Daniel Griswold. "Immigrants Have Enriched American Culture and Enhanced Our Influence in the World." *Cato Institute.* Cato Institute, 18 Feb. 2002. Web. 5 July 2017.

2. Jeffrey M. Jones. "In U.S., 65% Favor Path to Citizenship for Illegal Immigrants." *Gallup.* Gallup, 12 Aug. 2015. Web. 5 July 2017.

3. "Immigrants' Rights: What's At Stake." *American Civil Liberties Union.* ACLU, 2017. Web. 5 July 2017.

CHAPTER 8. THE CASE AGAINST IMMIGRATION

1. "Foreign-Born Workers: Labor Force Characteristics—2016." *News Release Bureau of Labor Statistics.* US Department of Labor, 18 May 2017. Web. 5 July 2017.

2. Gustavo López and Jynnah Radford. "Statistical Portrait of the Foreign-Born Population in the United States." *Hispanic Trends.* Pew Research Center, 3 May 2017. Web. 5 July 2017.

3. Bernadette D. Proctor, Jessica L. Semega, and Melissa A. Kollar. "Income and Poverty in the United States: 2015." *US Census Bureau.* US Census Bureau, 20 Apr. 2017. Web. 5 July 2017.

4. Tal Kopan. "What Donald Trump Has Said about Mexico and Vice Versa." *CNN: Politics.* Turner Broadcasting System, 31 Aug. 2016. Web. 5 July 2017.

5. Sara Kehaulani Goo. "What Americans Want to Do about Illegal Immigration." *Fact Tank.* Pew Research Center, 24 Aug. 2015. Web. 5 July 2017.

6. Ibid.

7. Thomas B. Edsall. "What Does Immigration Actually Cost Us?" *New York Times.* New York Times, 29 Sept. 2016. Web. 5 July 2017.

8. Jie Zong and Jeanne Batalova. "Frequently Requested Statistics on Immigrants and Immigration in the United States." *Migration Information Source.* Migration Policy Institute, 8 Mar. 2017. Web. 5 July 2017.

9. Mary Tamer. "The Education of Immigrant Children." *Usable Knowledge.* Harvard Graduate School of Education, 11 Dec. 2014. Web. 5 July 2017.

10. Genevieve Wood. "Undocumented Children a Drain on U.S. Schools." *Heritage Foundation.* Heritage Foundation, 9 Sept. 2014. Web. 5 July 2017.

11. Gustavo López and Kristen Bialik. "Key Findings About U.S. Immigrants." *Fact Tank.* Pew Research Center, 3 May 2017. Web. 5 July 2017.

12. Eric Bradner. "7 Lines That Defined Trump's Immigration Speech." *CNN: Politics.* Turner Broadcasting System, 1 Sept. 2016. Web. 5 July 2017.

CHAPTER 9. LOOKING AHEAD

1. "Modern Immigration Wave Brings 59 Million to U.S., Driving Population Growth and Change Through 2065." *Hispanic Trends.* Pew Research Center, 28 Sept. 2015. Web. 5 July 2017.

2. Ibid.

3. Pascal-Emmanuel Gobry. "6 Immigration Reform Ideas That Would Actually Work." *Business.* Forbes, 20 Mar. 2013. Web. 5 July 2017.

INDEX

ABOUT THE
AUTHOR

A. R. Carser is a freelance writer who lives in Minnesota. She enjoys learning and writing about US history, culture, and society.